1 MONTH OF
FREE
READING

at

www.ForgottenBooks.com

By purchasing this book you are eligible for one month membership to ForgottenBooks.com, giving you unlimited access to our entire collection of over 1,000,000 titles via our web site and mobile apps.

To claim your free month visit: www.forgottenbooks.com/free912257

ISBN 978-0-265-93557-6
PIBN 10912257

NOTES

ON

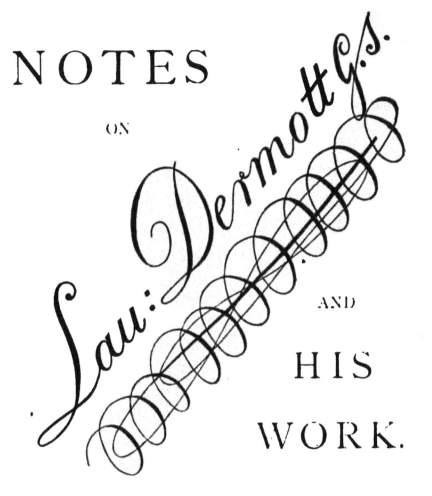

AND

HIS

WORK.

BY

WITHAM MATTHEW BYWATER, P.M. No. 19.

LONDON.

1884.

hib

[Privately Printed.]

DEDICATED

TO MY

BRETHREN

OF

"*ANTIENT*" DESCENT.

PREFACE.

IN presenting the following pages* to the notice of my Brethren, it is right I should explain, that when looking about for material with which to sketch a brief history of my Lodge at its Centenary in 1869, I was permitted by the kindness of the late Grand Secretary, Brother John Hervey, to examine the old books which formerly belonged to the Grand Lodge of the "Antient" Masons. The contents so greatly interested me, not only as affording information of the general business of that body, but as illustrating the Masonic career of a Brother who contributed so largely by his zeal to advance the cause of Masonry in the last century, that I was led to make more copious notes than otherwise were required for the immediate object I had then in view.

* Read before the Members of the Royal Athelstan Lodge, No. 19, May 1884.

In his lifetime, and in the brief notices which have since occasionally appeared, I venture to think Laurence Dermott has been somewhat roughly treated, and motives have been imputed to him which recorded events scarcely justify. As a zealous and consistent upholder of Masonic law, it was no small honour—it must have been a source of gratification—to him, during his long tenure of office, to have furthered the interests of Masonry by his devotion, both as regards time and labour, to the duties which fell to him to discharge.

In submitting the following " Notes on Laurence Dermott and his Work," it is my desire to present him as he appears in the old records, where, by his work and his manner of doing it, he may plead for himself, until a competent writer shall do justice to his memory and fame.

W. M. B.

5, *Hanover Square, W.* .
December 5th, 1884.

NOTES ON LAURENCE DERMOTT

AND HIS WORK.

THE prosperity and amazing growth of Free-masonry in England, as manifested by its having quadrupled the number of its Lodges within the present generation, is a constant theme of wonder. It has so far exceeded the expectations of the most sanguine of a former generation, that we are led to regard the struggles of the last century with no little degree of interest; and as ofttimes, apparent evils ultimately are productive of unexpected benefits, so the spirit of opposition which was then engendered was destined to work a positive good to the Craft. Thus sympathies were evoked and attention given to an Institution which otherwise might have been regarded but with indifference.

Leaving to the speculative mind the task of weighing probabilities and determining what might have been the condition of Masonry to-day had not the Schism of 1738 awakened a feeling of emulation, and whether the apathy and lethargy of a preceding age might not otherwise have been reproduced, we will proceed to consider the events which exercised the minds of our Brethren in those days, and strengthened the foundation for the work which is now being so successfully carried on, under the patronage of our illustrious Grand Master.

We are reminded by the author of " Ahiman Rezon " that " it has been the general custom of all my Worthy Brethren who have honoured the Craft with their Books . . . for Free Masons to give us a long and pleasing History of Masonry from the Creation to the Time of their writing and publishing such accounts." It is therefore with a sense of relief that, for our present purpose, a retrospective glance beyond the last century is unnecessary. The circumstances immediately preceding the Schism need be merely alluded to, as they are fairly well known to most enquiring Masons. Many time-honoured misstatements, complacently repeated by almost every writer of the old school, were for a long time accepted as history; but thanks to Brothers Gould, Hughan, Norton, Whytehead and others, to all of whom we are so deeply indebted for the new light which their investigations are shedding upon the past, many illusions are being dispelled and new facts by degrees revealed. It may be briefly stated that the revival of Freemasonry in the South of

England was brought about in 1717, when the four existing Lodges constituted themselves a Grand Lodge, under the title of "The Grand Lodge of England," as distinctive from the York Masons, who designated themselves "The Grand Lodge of *all* England." The Grand Lodge in the South became a flourishing body, not undisturbed however by occasional discord, which it is no part of our business to discuss here. But in 1738 many worthy Masons, being dissatisfied with certain irregularities and innovations which they averred were contrary to ancient Masonry, and after much discontent formed themselves into a separate Grand Lodge. Their proceedings soon had the sympathy and approval of the Grand Lodges of Scotland and Ireland, who gave them countenance and support. "To disappoint the views of these deluded Brethren, and to distinguish the persons initiated by them, the Grand Lodge (of England) readily acquiesced in the imprudent measures which the regular Masons had adopted; measures which even the urgency of the case could not warrant." The result was soon evident. The seceding Brethren of Grand Lodge now styled themselves "ANTIENT" Masons, in accordance with the accepted appellation of the York Grand Lodge, and designated the Brethren who had introduced the *new* plans, "Modern" Masons, which terms have long distinguished the two

B

Grand Lodges.* We have few records to en-
lighten us on the disputed points. The chief
writer who has handed down to us the history
of those times was William Preston. He was initiated in an Antient Lodge, No. 111, in 1763. That
Lodge was re-constituted under the " Moderns "
in 1764, and adopted the name of " Caledonian,"
which it still retains, being now No. 134. This
secession from the ranks of the " Antients,"
together with an angry correspondence, which
will be hereafter referred to, was not calculated
to conduce to an *impartial* history of " Antient "
Masonry from the pen of William Preston, whose
mind was doubtless warped to no small degree
by these events; and we must feel, that if history
is to have a practical value, it must be handed
down to us without bias or partiality. Preston
quitted the ranks of the " Antients " and became
an adopted member of the " Moderns;" but his
career was not altogether an undisturbed one.
Having already censured the " Antients " for their
secession, he was (with some of his Brethren)
expelled from his adopted Grand Lodge in 1779,
for disavowing allegiance to it; averring that his

* It has been erroneously stated that Dermott gave these
names, " *Modern* " and " *Antient,*" to the two Grand Lodges.
These names were introduced in 1739, whereas Dermott
was not initiated until 1740, and does not appear to have
arrived in England until *after* 1746.

Lodge (the Lodge of Antiquity) derived its rights from the Grand Lodge of York, and was therefore of more antient descent than that of the Grand Lodge of 1717. Thus the events of 1738 were repeated in 1779. He and his Brethren continued in that enforced state of expulsion for eleven years, at the expiration of which period, wiser counsels prevailed, and the Lodge of Antiquity was restored to its original position on the roll of its Grand Lodge. The effect of keen rivalry was soon evident; and the two Grand Lodges, thus stimulated to more active exertions, prospered accordingly. It has been said that to the slightly tilting of the earth's axis, the beauty and variety of days and seasons are due; and in like manner, the divergence of opinions among the Masons of that day, brought about a result which more level tendencies would have failed to accomplish so thoroughly.

It is, however, with the "Antient" Masons that our interest lies, and to that body only these remarks will be confined. Once firmly established, the Brethren held meetings, constituted Lodges, and enrolled members. They were ruled by a Grand Committee presided over by a Master, selected in rotation according to the number of his Lodge, a new Chairman being appointed for each meeting; and this arrangement continued in force for fifteen years. It is doubtful whether they preserved any minutes or records of their proceedings before 1751, when the existing records commence, which consist of Grand Lodge and Stewards' Lodge Minutes, and Register of Lodges; and it is from this quarry chiefly that the following notes have been taken.

From this date onward, for a period of about forty years, the conduct of the business of the Antient Grand Lodge, and the future success of the Order, were greatly influenced and controlled by the fire and energy of a man who has no superior in its annals, and who now comes upon the scene.

Laurence Dermott was an Irishman, and was born in 1720. He was initiated in Ireland in 1740, and having served all the offices, including that of Secretary, was installed W.M. of No. 26, Dublin, June 24th, 1746. He was a man of considerable capacity and of some social proclivities; and at an early age he came to London, with perhaps little money in his purse, but many projects in his head. The elements for a story are slight, as the " Transactions " do not supply many particulars of him; but the facts recorded there are sufficient to render him conspicuous amongst his fellows. We may suppose he was fairly well educated for those days, as is attested by the correspondence which occasionally appears on its pages; while his firm and vigorous handwriting is indicative of his character, which was energy—frequently resisted, but nevertheless, energy irresistible. He lectured frequently

AHIMAN REZON:

OR,

A Help to a Brother;

Shewing the

EXCELLENCY of SECRECY,

And the first Cause, or Motive, of the Institution of

FREE-MASONRY;

THE

PRINCIPLES of the CRAFT,

And the

Benefits arising from a strict Observance thereof;
What Sort of MEN ought to be initiated into the MYSTERY,
And what sort of MASONS are fit to govern LODGES,
With their Behaviour in and out of the Lodge.

Likewise the

Prayers used in the *Jewish* and *Christian* Lodges,

The Ancient Manner of

Constituting new Lodges, with all the Charges, &c.

Also the

OLD and NEW REGULATIONS,

The Manner of Chusing and Installing *Grand-Master* and *Officers*
and other useful Particulars too numerous here to mention.

To which is added,

The greatest Collection of MASONS SONGS ever presented to
public View, with many entertaining PROLOGUES and EPILOGUES;

Together with

SOLOMON's TEMPLE an ORATORIO,

As it was performed for the Benefit of

FREE-MASONS.

LONDON:
ted for the EDITOR, and sold by Brother *James Bedford*, at th
Crown in St. *Paul's* Church-Yard.

on Masonic subjects, and he wrote songs. It was the custom of the time to include songs at the end of Masonic books, and so he adopted the custom. Not only did he write songs, but he sang them to his brethren ; perhaps feeling that

"A verse may finde him, who a sermon flies."

In 1756 he achieved literary fame by producing a book which will hand down his name to all time. He entitled it "Ahiman Rezon," or, "A Help to a Brother." Various interpretations of it have been given. Dr. Crucifix renders it "a corruption of three Hebrew words—achi, man, ratson—signifying 'the thoughts or opinions of a true and faithful Brother.'" It was immediately accepted as the Book of Constitutions of the Antients. This book went through several editions, and became the model for many similar works in other countries. Brother Carson of Cincinnati, in his valuable and interesting "Masonic Bibliography," thus alludes to the work and its author :—" The Ahiman Razon is one of the most famous books in connexion with Masonic literature ; it was the 'law-book' of the 'Ancients,' in contradistinction to Anderson's 'Book of Constitutions,' the book of the 'Moderns.' Dermott was the literary man of the 'Ancients.' Ireland, Pennsylvania, Maryland and South Carolina have entitled their Book of Constitution 'Ahiman Rezon.'"

We know little of his circumstances. It may be inferred that his means were very limited when he arrived in England. About two years afterwards, he describes himself as being in the employment of a master painter. Later on, his circumstances improved, and we find him contributing £5 5s. to a fund in aid of a distressed Brother, also £10 to the Charity. Then came the gout and its miseries, indicating perhaps less active employment and a more liberal rule of living. He is subsequently described as a Wine-merchant in the City of London, and his zeal for Masonry led him to present his Grand Lodge with a throne, which cost him a considerable sum. With the good nature of advancing years, he also gave all his interest in the " Ahiman Rezon " for the benefit of the Charity. This prosperity would be the natural outcome of an active and industrious life—accustomed to work at his trade twelve hours a day, at the same time discharging the many duties connected with the Masonic offices which he continuously filled. His Masonic ability was great, and his knowledge of Craft and Royal Arch was considerable. Lecturing frequently, installing officers, adjudicating continually, combatting with opponents and refuting false charges, which in those less courteous days were continually preferred against him ; for in spite of his good qualities, it was part of his nature, by his vigorous and straightforward conduct, to bring upon himself adverse criticisms, and to provoke jealousies and aversions which have lasted to the present day. He was certainly not "mealy-mouthed," some of his replies being pungent, not a little acrimonious, but always incisive, especially in matters concerning the regularity of proceedings of Grand Lodge. This independence of thought and action, which he thus asserted so freely within certain limits, enabled him to exercise an extraordinary influence over Grand Lodge; and the great success of the Antients at this time, was due in a large measure to the untiring zeal of Dermott, who for so many years swayed its rulings, ever impelling it forward, staunch for its rights and the old traditions of Masonry.

Notwithstanding the haziness which envelopes his life, he seems to have been a good citizen; and as his sympathies were with William Pitt, we may conclude he was a supporter of Church and State as accepted in those days. There is a strain of genuine feeling about the man, obscured as it may be by this distance of time; and from his first appearance on the scene, forward through a long course of years, his name and his work in Grand Lodge sufficiently attest to the earnestness of his labours, entitling him to a better recognition at the hands of his Brethren than he has yet received.

Our first introduction to him is in Grand Committee, held February 5th, 1752, at the *Griffin*,

Holborn. For some years it had met at the *Turk's Head, Greek Street, Soho,* under the title of "The Grand Lodge of Free and Accepted Masons of the Old Constitutions." On the present occasion Mr. James Haggarty, Master of No. 4, presided, and there were also present "the officers of Nos. 2, 3, 4, 5, 6, 7, 8, 9 and 10, being the representatives of all the Antient Masons in and adjacent to London." Behold then Laurence Dermott, now a man of about thirty-two years of age. "On arriving in England he first joined a Modern Lodge," but he is now a member of No. 9 Lodge of the "Antients," also of No. 10,* at that time held at the *Red Lyon, Cross Lane, Long Acre.* Dermott also ranked as P.M. of No. 26, Ireland. The office of Grand Secretary having become vacant by the retirement of Brother John Morgan, Dermott was elected to it, and thereupon was "installed in the antient manner." Brother Morgan then gave up the books, Dermott being solemnly bound over never to deliver certain MSS.—described as being a large folio, bound in vellum—"to any person but him, the said John Morgan, or his order in writing." It is difficult to say what were the other books now given up, as on a subsequent occasion the Grand Secretary records that "he never received any copy or manuscript of

---

° In 1792 the Royal Athelstan Lodge, then No. 159, was permitted to purchase the vacant No. 10, which it retained until the Union, when it became No. 19.

the former Transactions from Mr. Morgan, lately Grand Secretary, nor does the present Grand Secretary think that Br. John Morgan did keep any Book of Transactions in this form, though there is no certainty he did not."

Having been thus installed into office, his records of proceedings in Grand Committee are at times extremely interesting and amusing. On the next day of meeting, the following appears in Dermott's handwriting, under date March 4th, 1752:—" Complaints made against Thomas Phealon and John Mackey, better known by the name of 'leg of mutton Masons.' In course of examination it appeared that Phealon and Mackey had initiated many persons for the consideration of a leg of Mutton for dinner or supper, to the disgrace of the Ancient Craft. That Mackey was an Empiric in Physic, and both imposters in Masonry. That upon examining some Brothers whom they pretended to have made Royal Arch* men, the parties had not the least idea of that Secret. That Dr. Mackey pretended to teach a Masonical Art by which any man could (in a moment) render himself Invisible. That the Grand Secretary had examined Mackey, who appeared incapable of making an apprentice with any degree of propriety. Nor had Mackey the least Idea or knowledge of Royal Arch Masonry. But instead thereof, he had told the

---

* This is the first mention of the " Royal Arch " in the books of the " Antient " Grand Lodge.

people whom he had deceived a long story about 12 white Marble stones, &c., &c., and that the Rain Bow was the Royal Arch, with many Other Absurdities equally foreign and Rediculous."

There is a foot-note on this page : "This was the first time that Laurenee Dermott acted as principal Secretary; nor did he take any fees before the 27th April, 1752."

The next entry is dated April 1, 1752, when the Grand Committee met at the *Griffin, Holborn*. The copy of the Bye-laws for private Lodges, as written by the late Grand Secretary, J. Morgan, was read and compared with Br. L. Dermott's copy of Bye-laws of his former Lodge, No. 26 in the City of Dublin, and the latter being deemed the most correct, it was "Resolved to adopt them, &c." Thanks voted to Philip McLoughlin and J. Morgan, for their trouble, &c., in drawing up the former Bye-laws. John Morgan, James Hagan, and L. Dermott reported that they had waited upon Lord George Sackvile, but he replied he had to proceed to Ireland, and also that he had just been elected G.M. of Ireland. That on his retnrn he would accept the Chair, or recommend another "Noble Man."

The Grand Committee met again at the *Griffin, Holborn*, on May 6, 1752. Motion made that this Grand Committee be removed back to the *Turk's Head* in Greek Street, Soho, where it had long been held under the Title of "The Grand Lodge of Free and Accepted Masons of the Old Constitutions." Not seconded, and therefore dropped. It was then resolved to remove to "The Temple Eating House, the sign of the *Temple* in *Shire Lane*,* near Temple Bar, London."

Accordingly, on June 3, 1752, the Grand Committee met at the *Temple, Shire Lane*, when, having no Grand Master or Grand Wardens to install, the Grand Secretary was re-installed according to the antient custom of installing Grand Secretaries, and he was proclaimed and saluted; "after which he repeated the whole ceremony of installing Grand Officers, &c., in the manner which he had learned from Br. Edward Spratt, the celebrated Grand Secretary of Ireland."

In Grand Committee, July 1, 1752.—Heard complaint, and ordered Br. Willoughby to refund nine shillings to a Brother whom he had wronged. "Whereupon Br. Moses Willoughby declared they might expell him, for he would not conform to the rules of any Society upon Earth by which he should lose nine shillings. Expelled accordingly."

August 5, 1752.—"The Grand Secretary again urged the necessity of chusing a Grand Mr. Upon

---

* Shire Lane or Sheer Lane commenced on the north side of Temple Bar, and ran across the site of the new Courts of Justice. In earlier times it divided London from the fields, hence its name of Shire Lane.

which the Worshipful Master in the Chair made an Excellent Speech, wherein he labour'd to fire the Brethren with a spirit to Pursue the Grand design : and concluded with saying, ' Future Ages will bless your memories for preserving and reviving the Antient Craft in England.' "

On the 2nd September, 1752, after the disposal of business of a financial nature, it was Resolved that this Grand Committee shall be formed immediately into a working Lodge of Master Masons, in order to hear a Lecture from the Grand Secretary, Laurence Dermott. The Lodge was opened in Antient form of Grand Lodge, and every part of real Freemasonry was traced and explained, except the Royal Arch. The Lecture ended and the Lodge was closed with the most agreeable and harmonious humour.

September 14, 1752.—Emergency at the *Temple*. Resolutions were adopted authorising the granting of Warrants and Dispensations for forming and holding Lodges, " otherwise the Antient Craft must dwindle into nothing." A foot-note states : " An Order of this sort was made in a General Assembly of Antient Masons at the *Turk's Head* Tavern in Greek Street, Soho, upon the 17th day of July, 1751, wherein the Masters of Nos. 2, 3, 4, 5, 6 and 7 were authorised to grant Dispensations and Warrants and to act as Grand Master, and the Masters of Nos. 3, 4, 5 and 6 did actually exercise authority in signing the warrant of No. 8 for holding a Lodge at the sign of the *Temple and Sun* in Shire Lane, Temple Bar, London, from which warrant this note is written; for Dermott never received any copy or manuscript of the former transactions from Mr. Morgan, late Grand Secretary, nor does Laurence Dermott, the present Grand Secretary, think that Brother John Morgan did keep any Book of Transactions in this form, though there is no certainty he did not."

A meeting was held at the *Temple*, Shire Lane, on the 6th of October, 1752, when a motion was made from the Chair, " That application be immediately made to some honourable Antient Brother to accept the honour of the Grand Mastership or Recommend us another." " Resolved, it is the unanimous opinion of Grand Committee that the Craft has flourished most and best when governed by a noble Grand Master. For though a General or Grand Committee have power to form new laws for the Fraternity, yet, to render them binding or render stability, a Grand Master is absolutely necessary to confirm them." It was finally arranged that every Brother should make due enquiries concerning proper persons, and report the result at the next meeting.

When they met on the 3rd of November following, " the names of several Noble and Honourable Gentlemen said to be Antient Masons " were laid before the Committee, and it was "Ordered that the Grand Secretary shall draw up a proper petition To the Right Honourable Philip Earl of Chesterfield, an Antient Mason, begging his Lordship's sanction as Grand Master." The Secretary returned thanks for the honour done him in appointing him the Committee to wait on Lord Chesterfield, and begged the Grand Committee would postpone the business until they had made choice of some proper place to receive and Install his Lordship, the *Temple* Eating House being very unfit for that business. The friends of the Landlord objected to the Grand Secretary's request. "Upon which there were many altercations on both sides, not fit to be written." The consequence and conclusion was that the matter was wholly postponed.

The next matter to be here noticed does not relate specially to Dermott, although there can be little doubt he cordially concurred in it. But it is interesting, as it explains the motive which prompted the Grand Lodge to grant vacant high numbers to Lodges lower down on the Registry.

On the 6th December, 1752, it was "Resolved unanimously that the Lodges who, by neglect or disobedience, have forfeited their Rank or Number, shall be discontinued on the Registry; and the Junior Lodges who have proved themselves faithful friends of the Ancient Craft shall henceforth bear

the Title or Number so forfeited, the distribution
to be according to Seniority." At this meeting,
after considerable discussion, it was resolved to
remove to the *Five Bells Tavern, Strand.* "The
Grand Secretary desired to know whether there
were any other Books or MSS. more than had
been delivered to him by the Worshipful Mr. James
Hagarty, the presiding Officer on the 2nd February, 1752, and Mr. John Morgan, late Grand
Secretary. To which several of the Brethren
answered that they did not know of any. Others
said that they knew Mr. Morgan had a Roll of
parchment of prodigious length, which contained
some Historical matters relative to the Antient
Craft, which parchment they did suppose he had
taken abroad with him. It was further said that
many MSS. were lost amongst the Lodges lately
' Modernized,' where a vestige of the Antient Craft
was not suffered to be revived or practized, and it
was for this reason so many of them withdrew
from Lodges (under the Modern sanction) to support the true Antient System. That they found
the Freemasons from Ireland and Scotland had
been Initiated in the very same manner as themselves, which confirmed their system and practice
as right and just, without which none could be
deemed legal, though possessed of all the Books
and Papers on Earth. The Grand Secretary
(Dermott) produced a very old MS., written or

copied by one Bramhall of Canterbury, in the reign of King Henry VII., which MS. was presented to Brother Dermott (in 1748) by one of the descendants of the writer. On perusal it proved to contain the whole matter in the 'forementioned parchment, as well as other matters not in that parchment. The Grand Secretary expatiated much on the subject of this old MS., to the great satisfaction of the hearers, and on his conclusion a motion was made for the thanks of the Grand Committees to be given to the G.S. Dermott 'for the many pleasing instructions which he had so often administered to the Brethren;' upon which four Brethren protested against any thanks or even approbation of the Secretary's conduct, who, instead of being useful, had actually sung and lectured the Brethren out of their senses, and had then proposed to move the Grand Committee out of the house of a worthy Brother to the house of a man who was not a Mason. . . . As soon as the paper containing the above protest was publickly read and copied, the Secretary begged to be heard in answer to the Landlord and his friends. This request being granted, the Secretary said that he did not desire to continue in office longer than he should be found useful . . . and if he was so unfortunate as to sing any Brother out of his senses, he hoped the W.M. in the Chair and the Grand Committee would allow him an hour's time, and he would endeavour to sing them into their senses again. The request was granted with great good humour, the Secretary made good use of his time, and the W.M. closed, &c., &c."

Nothing occurs demanding notice until July 13, 1753, when an Emergency was held at the *King and Queen*, Cable Street, Rosmary Lane, when we find recorded—" The Grand Secretary humbly begged that the Lodge would please to appoint some certain person to deliver the summons's for the future, that he the s^d Secretary was under the necessity of delivering or paying for delivery for some months past, as he was obliged to work twelve hours in the day for the Master Painter who employed him." Clearly shewing that at that period Dermott was in very humble circumstances. It was ultimately ordered that the Grand Tyler or the Grand Pursuivant should deliver the summonses. The Worshipful Master in the Chair thanked the Grand Secretary for the last new song which he had composed, and " hoped that the applause of his Brethren would induce Br. Dermott, G.S., to compose another against the next St. John's-day ;" which the Grand Secretary promised to attempt.

The next mention of Dermott's name appears under date October 18, 1753, when it was " Proposed and agreed, That the Grand Secretary shall attend and regulate all processions, and at Funerals take particular care that all persons walk in proper rotation." It was also "Proposed 'that Bro. Burgoyne shall have a petition to go round the Antient Lodges.' The Grand Secretary made a long speech against such petitions, and being put to vote it was carried in the negative."

Hitherto, as recorded in these old minutes, the Masters of Lodges presided over the Grand Committees in rotation, according to the Number of the Lodge, a new Chairman being appointed at each meeting. Henceforth a new order of things commenced: a Grand Master ruled the body; the meetings ceased to be designated Grand Committees, and were constituted a Grand Lodge.

At a meeting held at the *Bells Tavern*, December 5, 1753, Mr. Lachlan McIntosh, Master of No. 3, in the Chair, "The Grand Secretary made a motion, 'That as the Fraternity had not made choice of any of the Noble personages formerly mentioned in those Transactions, and it being doubtful whether the Antient Craft could be honoured with a Noble Grand Master at this time, he humbly begged that the Brethren would make choice of some worthy and skilfull Master to fill the Chair for the space of six months successively.' Accordingly, Brother Robert Turner, Master of No. 15, was nominated and unanimously chosen its first Grand Master.*

* The line of Antient Grand Masters thus commenced, continued until the Union in 1813, on which occasion H.R.H. The Duke of Kent (father of Her Most Gracious Majesty) occupied that distinguished position.

Installed and saluted, 'his Worship chose Br. W. Rankin for his Deputy, who was also immediately installed and saluted . . . Then the Lodge proceeded in the choice of Grand Wardens, when Bro. S. Quay, P.M. No. 2, was chosen Senior Grand Warden, and Br. L. McIntosh, of No. 3, was chosen Junior Grand Warden, who were also installed and saluted according to Antient Usage; and concluded with the most agreeable harmony.'"

On the 6th February, 1754, Grand Lodge having been opened in ample Form, and various matters of business disposed of, a jewel was voted to Grand Secretary Laurence Dermott for his great services. The jewel was to be his own property, and not that of Grand Lodge; nevertheless, a foot-note states— "Dermott delivered the Jewell to his successor, Mr. William Dickey, and was worn by succeeding Grand Secretaries."

On the 14th March, 1754, a Grand Committee of Masters only was held at the *Thistle and Crown*, Church Court, Strand, the Grand Master being in the Chair. On recommendation of the Grand Secretary, it was resolved to hold a Monthly Committee of Masters at *The Crown*, St. Paul's Churchyard, under the name of Committee of Inspection, to consider the merits of petitions for charity.

On June 5, 1754, a very serious charge having been proved against John Hamilton, he was turned down stairs, and orders were issued to prevent his admission into any Antient Lodge.

At a Grand Lodge, held Sept. 4, 1754, it was ordered " That all our monthly meetings shall be published in the *Daily Advertiser*, with the Grand Secretary L. Dermott's name annexed ; that the said Secretary shall draw up such advertisements as prudence shall direct him, and the expenses attending such publications shall be re-imbursed to him the said Secretary on every Grand Lodge meeting."

At the following meeting (Oct. 2, 1754), on the recommendation of Dermott, a set of Grand Lodge Jewels were ordered ; at the same time, the Grand Secretary returned thanks for the jewel voted to him Feb. 6 last.

Grand Lodge held at *The Bells*, Nov. 6, 1754— It was resolved to call the Committee of Charity, henceforth, " THE STEWARDS' LODGE." It was also ordered " That the Grand Lodge cease meeting on the first Wednesday in every Kallendar month, and in future to meet on first Wednesdays in March, June, September and December, and on both St. John's days yearly."

December 27, 1754.—Brother Edward Vaughan was Installed Grand Master.

At a Grand Lodge held on Dec. 27, 1755, being St. John's-day, for the Installation of Grand Master, the following memorandum was made by Laurence Dermott :—" This year 1755, the *Modern* Masons began to make use of Certificates ; though the

Antient Masons had granted Certificates time immemorial."

Grand Lodge, June 2, 1756.—A warm discussion arose relative to the source whence funds should be obtained for the purchase of Candlesticks. "The Grand Secretary begged an audience, which, being granted, he said he would propose a scheme by w^h they w^d be enabled to purchase (even Silver) Candlesticks, without drawing anything out of the Grand Lodge Funds nor any contribution from the Lodges. This was rec^d with applause, and an explanation required; upon which the Grand Secretary observed that Warrants were granted (for the holding of Lodges) at the small expense of the Secretary's fees, and he therefore humbly proposed that One Guinea should be levied on every new Warrant for the future." Unanimously agreed to. Ordered, " that the thanks of this Grand Lodge shall be given to our Grand Secretary for his Excellent proposal, and intreat him to continue in the study of the Interest and Honour of the Antient Craft."

June 24, 1756.—The Grand Secretary was ordered to attend various Lodges to install.

On the 27th December, 1756, "the R^t Honble William Stuart, Earl of Blesington, was installed (by proxy) Grand Master."

Grand Lodge, March 2, 1757.—Heard an appeal from John Hamilton, an excluded member (see June 5, 1754), setting forth the unhappiness of his

mind and the many injuries which he had received
through his being excluded from all Lodges, and
most humbly desired to be admitted for a few
moments, when he would make it appear that sen-
tence against him was not only cruel but also un-
just. After many debates the said John Hamilton
was admitted, and being ordered to fulfil what he
had asserted in his Appeal, " He said that the
former complaints against him were all groundless
and malicious, and carried against him by the
cunning and wickedness of an Imposter, viz.,
Laurence Dermott, the Secretary, who had imposed
on the whole Craft in saying that he was regularly
made in Ireland, &c., whereas the said Dermott
was only a clandestine Mason, made by James
Hagan and others at a house in Long Acre, some
years before. That his whole drift was to keep the
Society in ignorance, and with his singing and
tricks to lull them on until they had accumulated a
considerable sum of money, and then to rob them.
The late Grand Master, E. Vaughan, Esq., stood
up and said he found himself very unhappy in
hearing such a vile character of the Grand Secretary, whom he had taken for a most deserving
Brother, and therefore earnestly moved the said
Secretary should be immediately ordered to make
his defence. This motion was put in execution,
when the Secretary arose and begged leave to read
a certain Regulation, which being granted, he read

as follows : ' If a complaint be made against a Brother by another Brother, and he be found guilty, he shall stand to the determination of the Lodge ; but if a complaint be made against a Brother, wherein the Accuser cannot support his complaint to conviction, such Accuser shall forfeit such penalty as the person so accused might have forfeited had he been really convicted on such complaint.' Then the Grand Secretary addressed himself to the Chair and said : ' Right Worshipful Sir and Brethren,—This is the Antient and most equitable law made and observed by our ancestors, always approved and confirmed by you, and therefore by this Law I stand or fall.' To which the Right Worshipful in the Chair replied : ' As the Law of Masons has decreed, so shall all things here be done.' Then his Worship called on the Accuser and told him he must prove his assertion. The Accuser ordered James Hagan before the Lodge, who, being asked whether he did make Lau : Dermott (G.S.) a Freemason, he answered and declared ' he did not, neither did he ever teach him anything relative to Masonry, nor could he devise what reason Mr. Hamilton had for saying so.' The Grand Master then asked Mr. Hamilton if he had any other person to call on this occasion, upon which Lau : Rooke arose and said that he verily believed that Br. John Hamilton's accusation , was true. Being asked his reason for thinking so, he answered, because Br. Hamilton told him so, and at the same time swore to it in such a manner as to leave no doubt behind."

Then the Grand Secretary was ordered to make his final defence. He addressed the Grand Lodge and said: "Right Worshipful Grand Master, and the rest of my worthy Brethren here assembled,— By my conduct hitherto, I hope you are convinced that I have not done you any wrong. As to my intention of robbing you . . . this must be left to the great tell-tale Time, it being impossible to convince this Lodge as to my present way of thinking, much less what I may think in future. And as to the other charge of imposing on you and being made in a clandestine manner in London, I shall beg leave to have the present and past Masters of No. 2 examined on that head, and I humbly and earnestly beg that the said Master and Past-Masters may be put to the Master Mason's test on this occasion."

Then arose Br. Thomas Allen, P.M. No. 2, and proved that Br. Dermott had faithfully served all offices in a very respectable Lodge held in his house in the City of Dublin, which servitude was prior to the said Dermott's coming to England; and further declared that he never heard any crime (in or out of the Lodge) laid to his charge. Br. Charles Byrne, Senr., W.M. of No. 2, proved that Laurence Dermott having faithfully served the

Offices of Senior and Junior Deacon, Senior and Junior Warden, and Secretary, was by him regularly installed Master of the Good Lodge No. 26 in the Kingdom of Ireland, upon the 24th day of June, 1746; and that all these transactions were prior to Mr. Dermott's coming to England.

Lastly, Br. Dermott produced a Certificate (signed " Edward Spratt, Grand Secretary") under the seal of the Grand Lodge of Ireland, of his good behaviour and servitude, &c., &c., which gave entire satisfaction, upon which the Grand Lodge came to the following resolution: " Resolved, it is the opinion of this Grand Lodge that John Hamilton, late of No. 19, is unworthy of being admitted into a Mason's Lodge or any other good Society; and therefore it is hereby ordered that the said John Hamilton shall not be admitted within the door of any Antient Lodge during his Life; and the said John Hamilton having been several times excluded for malpractices and again reinstated, yet still continues in his vile offences, of which clandestine makings are not the least."

It may be here noted that at this same meeting it was ordered " that a General Meeting of Master Masons be held on the 13th inst., to compare and regulate several things relative to the Antient Craft which cannot be committed to writing. That the Masters of the Royal Arch shall also be summoned

E

to meet, in order to regulate things relative to that most valuable branch of the Craft."*

Accordingly, a Grand Lodge of Emergency was held on the 13th March, 1757, when it is recorded that "the Grand Secretary, L. Dermott, called on a certain number of the Masters to attend the Grand Master's orders and work the Lodge." "In the course of this business the Grand Secretary traced and explained the 1st, 2nd and 3rd part of the Antient Craft, and settled many things (then disputed) to the entire satisfaction of all the Brethren present, who faithfully promised to adhere strictly to the Antient system and to cultivate the same in their several Lodges." Twenty-five of the forty-six Lodges then meeting in London were represented on this occasion.

On June 1, 1757, it was ordered "That if any Master, Warden or Presiding Officer, or any other person whose business it may be to admit members or visitors, screen, admit, harbour or entertain in his or their Lodge or Lodges during Lodge hours or the time of transacting the proper business of Freemasonry, any Mason (member or visitor) not

* A writer, in allusion to the Royal Arch, says:—"It is, in fact, the second part of the old Masters' grade, which Dermott made use of to mark a supposed difference as between 'ancients' and 'moderns.' Where he got the name 'Royal Arch' from, is not quite clear."

strictly an 'Antient' Mason, conformable to the Grand Lodge's rules and orders (certified sojourners only excepted), such Lodge so transgressing shall forfeit their Warrant, and the same may be disposed of the next Grand or Steward's Lodge."

March 1758.—Letter from Mr. John Calder, Grand Secretary in Dublin, was read, wherein he assured Grand Lodge of Antient Masons in London that the Grand Lodge of Ireland did mutually concur in a strict union with the Antient Grand Lodge in London, and promised to keep a constant correspondence with them.

On June 6, 1759, the following receipt relative to the Candlesticks appears :—" Received, June 6, 1759, from Mr. L. Dermott, £43 for five mahogany Candlesticks, made according to the Five Orders of Columns. By me, John Byrne."

An interesting foot-note occurs under date Dec. 16, 1759, to the effect that one Carroll, a distressed Mason from Ireland, petitioned the Modern Masons (not knowing the difference), and that Mr. Spence, then Secretary to the Modern Society, sent out an answer, viz., "Your being an Antient Mason, you are not entitled to any of our Charity. The Antient Masons have a Lodge at the *Five Bells* in the Strand, &c. Our Society is neither Arch, Royal-Arch, or Antient, so that you have no right to partake of our Charity."

A Grand Lodge was held Dec. 27, 1760, when

Thomas Erskine, Earl of Kelly, was installed Grand
Master. On that occasion " Grand Lodge unanimously ordered that Br. George Donovan shall
stand upon the middle table, and shall there audibly
read a certain paper given to him for that purpose,
as follows: " The Grand Lodge of Antient Masons,
truly sensible of the eminent and disinterested services done by their Secretary, Laurence Dermott,
have this day thought proper to order the general
thanks of the Fraternity to be given to him, the
said Laurence Dermott; and that this Resolution
shall be recorded in our Transactions, not only as
a testimony of our approbation and high esteem,
but also as an encouragement to future Secretaries
to endeavour to imitate him." The Grand Secretary, in his place, told the Grand Master and the
Fraternity " that the extravagancy of the last resolution in favour of his conduct had surprised him
so much, that he was totally incapable of making a
suitable answer; nevertheless, the Grand Lodge
would do him strict justice in believing two things,
viz., that he thought himself as happy in his Secretaryship as the Great Pitt was in being Secretary
of State; 2ndly, that he would exert his utmost
powers for the good of the Antient Fraternity so
long as he lived."

On the 24th June, 1761, a motion was passed
thanking the Grand Secretary Dermott " for his
unwearied diligence and eminent services to the

Antient Fraternity;" after which he was saluted with five. He said it ought to have been three only. Debate followed. Grand Lodge resolved that any worthy Brother may be "drank or toasted as often as the Grand Lodge or Grand Master may determine;" and it was then resolved to toast the Grand Secretary with 39, being his 39th year; which was accordingly done. A foot-note, however, states that he was in his 41st year.

At an Emergency held on Sept. 26, 1761, a letter from Grand Master Lord Kelly was read, in which he excused his absence from Grand Lodge; after which his health was drank in form, and the Grand Secretary sang the Grand Master's Song.

On December 22, 1762, the spirit of discontent was again manifested, in a Grand Lodge of Emergency, by a complaint being made against Dermott, Grand Secretary, and others, charging them with collusion at a recent election for Warden, which charge was proved to be groundless.

On the 27th of the same month, "David Fisher, late G.W. elect, having attempted to form a Grand Lodge of his own, and offered to register Masons therein for sixpence each, was deemed unworthy of any office or seat in Grand Lodge."

At a Grand Lodge on March 2, 1763, Br. Robert Lockhead petitioned for a Dispensation to make Masons at the sign of the *White Hart* in the Strand, &c.; and a Dispensation was granted to him, to continue in force for the space of thirty days.

The following extract from the *Freemasons' Magazine*, January 1795, has reference to this Dispensation :—" Soon after William Preston arrived in London, a number of Brethren from Edinburgh resolved to institute a Freemasons' Lodge in this City, and applied to the Antient Grand Lodge in London, who immediately granted them a Dispensation. They met at the *White Hart*, Strand, and Mr. Preston was the second person who was Initiated under that Dispensation. The Lodge was soon after regularly constituted by the officers of the Antient Grand Lodge in person. It moved to the *Horn Tavern*, Fleet Street, then to *Scot's Hall*, Blackfriars, and then to the *Half Moon*, Cheapside, where it met for a considerable time. At length, Mr. Preston and other members having joined a Lodge under the English Constitution, at the *Talbot*, Strand, they prevailed on the rest of the Lodge at the *Half Moon* to petition for a Constitution. Lord Blaney, at that time Grand Master, readily acquiesced, and the Lodge was soon after constituted a second time, in ample form, by the name of ' The Caledonian Lodge.'"*

A dispute having arisen amongst the Brethren in

* With reference to this passage, see an interesting communication from Br. Jacob Norton, in the *Freemason* of 23rd July, 1881.

Birmingham, Dermott was authorised by Grand Lodge, on the 7th December, 1763, to proceed there to adjudicate thereon.

It having been resolved that a Treasurer be appointed, the election took place June 6th, 1764. Dermott was put in nomination, and " the officers of No. 31 gave notice that if the Secretary Dermott was chosen, they would give undeniable security for any trust reposed in him, not exceeding £1000." Dermott, however, declined, and Mr. Matthew Beath, No. 81, was elected to the new office.

March 5, 1766.—An agreement was made to form a procession, and wait upon the Grand Master (Lord Kelly). A foot-note informs us " The Grand Officers and others, in fourteen Coaches and Chariots, went in Masonical procession to his Lordship the Grand Master's House near Soho Square, and from thence through Hampstead and Highgate; back to dinner at the *Five Bells* Tavern, Strand."

In June following, a subscription was made for a Grand Warden, then in prison in Newgate awaiting his trial, to which Dermott gave Five Guineas. " It being the King's birthday, the Grand Lodge in due form drank the King's health as Master Masons."

On St. John's-day, June 24, 1766, the Grand Lodge was not opened, but " the Fraternity, by permission of the Grand Officers, met at the *Angell* in Whitechapel, and thence walked in procession to Stepney Church, where an excellent Sermon, founded on the general regulations of the Craft, was preached by the Rev. Mr. Parker Rowlands, our most worthy Brother. After the Sermon, the Fraternity, amounting to a vast number, with three Bands of Musick, walked in like manner to the *Angell* aforesaid, where they separated, and each Lodge went to dine at the Houses where held."

That Dermott was not the only musical Grand Officer, the following minute will show :—

September 3, 1766.—Heard complaint against Grand Warden Swan, for publishing a song reflecting on Br. William Dickey, Junr., entitled "The Swan and the Dickey Bird."

Earl Kelly being unable to attend Grand Lodge on account of his continued absence from London, Dermott informed Grand Lodge in December 1766, that he knew a fit and proper person for Grand Master, who was possessed of a forune of £16,000 per annum, but who could not be communicated with for two or three weeks. The Election was therefore postponed. We are subsequently informed that the extraordinary individual thus alluded to was the Honble. Thomas Matthews of Thomastown, Ireland, who, wherever he resided, whether in England, Ireland, France, &c., held a regular Lodge amongst his own domestics. He was also Prov. Grand Master for Munster.

At a Grand Lodge of Emergency held at the *Five Bells*, Strand, June 12, 1767, Grand Master

Matthews attended. A Sermon was ordered to be preached at the nearest Church (St. Clement's, in the Strand), on St. John's-day, and a dinner to be provided. "The Grand Secretary humbly desired that his Worship the Grand Master would be pleased to nominate the Text on which the Sermon was to be preached; to which the Right Worshipful answered in Latin: 'In principio erat sermo ille et sermo ille erat apud Deum eratque ille sermo Deus.' To which the Grand Secretary made a bow, and said: 'Fungor Officio meo.'" All went to St. Clement's on the 24th, excepting Dermott, who was confined to his bed with the gout; also the Grand Master, who was likewise absent from a similar cause.

"Ordered, that the Ringers of St. Clement's shall be paid one guinea, the poor of the Parish five guineas, and the Beadles ten shillings and sixpence."

Grand Lodge of Emergency, Nov. 25, 1767.— Heard complaint against the manner in which the Grand Master had been installed—without proper notice—and "that, in fact, he had been smuggled in." The D.G.M., in reply, explained that in times past it had frequently been the case that the Grand Master had been privately installed. "That the late Grand Master, Lord Blessington, was privately installed by the Grand Officers and Secretary, in his Lordship's Library in Margaret Street." The

F

Grand Master confirmed this statement, but stated his willingness to be re-installed, if it was the wish of Grand Lodge.

In December of the same year, the Grand Master informed the Grand Lodge that Br. Laurence Dermott, G.S., had made a voluntary gift of the Grand Master's Throne complete, which cost him £29 : 11 : 6, together with some other things, amounting in the whole to £34. "Ordered that the public thanks be returned to the donor."

About this time we have frequent entries— "G.S. Dermott absent in the Gout."

The customary march out took place on St. John's-day, June 24, 1768: "This day the Grand Officers and Brethren of other Lodges assembled at Deptford in Kent, where they heard an excellent Sermon preached by the Rev. Parker Rowlands, and from thence walked in Masonical procession to the Assembly Room on Blackheath, where they dined in form, but did not think proper to open the Grand Lodge."

[The first volume of the Transactions ends here
with the above pen and ink design, followed by an
Index of Contents, and Table of Fees as arranged
in 1751—57.]

The following relates to the Constitution of the Royal Athelstan Lodge, No. 19, and is given verbatim :—

"February 27, 1769.

" Grand Lodge opened at a ¾ before five oclock at the sign of the *Ship* in the Strand, Senior Grand Ward$^{n.}$ W. Clarke in the chair as Grand Master (for three hours only) by an Authority from the Worshipful Mr. W$^{m.}$ Dickey (Sen$^{r.}$) Deputy Grand Master. Pres$^{t.}$ J.G. Warden Christian, G Sect$^{y.}$ Dermott, D.G.Sect$^{y.}$ Dickey and members of warranted Lodges as under, James Irwin N$^{o.}$ 3, John Quigly N$^{o.}$ 27, Devon L Hookham N$^{o.}$ 63, W Bailey P.M Ch$^{s.}$ Adney. W$^{m.}$ Adney. Simeon Bailey — Goddard, Titcombe. John Bailey and John Burford N$^{o.}$ 93. Peter Stratwell P.M. Thos. Berridge N$^{o.}$ 144.

Constituted
Mr. Robt. Lockhead Master
Mr. James Inglis   Sen$^{r.}$ Warden
Mr. W$^{m.}$ Cousins   Jun$^{r.}$ Warden

Warrant N$^{o.}$ 159 Registered in Vol 6. Letter F page 289.

Closed at ¼ past 6 oclock and adjourned to the 1st Wednesday in March "

In the minutes of March 1, 1769, we find the name of " G$^{d.}$ Sect$^{y.}$ Dermott," wine-merchant, of

King Street, Tower Hill, put in nomination with others for the office of Deputy Grand Master.

Grand Lodge held June 6, 1770.—On a vote of thanks to W. Dickey, Junr., Deputy Grand Secretary, Br. Dermott asserted that Br. Dickey resigned his post "when he (Dermott) was so ill in the gout, that he was obliged to be carried out of his bed (when incapable to wear shoes, stockings or even britches) to do his duty at Gd. Steward's Lodge." He further complained that Dickey Junr. did pirate and publish a certain print, the property of him (Dermott). After angry discussion, it was proposed that Dermott and Dickey should shake hands. Dermott was willing, but Dickey declined. It was afterwards explained that Dermott had printed some tickets for the Grand Master's Feast, which he claimed as his private property. He now gave the Stewards of the Feast permission to use them for this occasion only, and he received the thanks of Grand Lodge, "after the manner of Master Masons." This unfortunate feeling did not end here, for at the following meeting, Sept. 5, Dermott again called attention to his dispute with Dickey Junr. and threatened to print his case. Nothing satisfactory having been arrived at, Dermott stated his intention of resigning all office in Grand Lodge.

These angry discussions were renewed at the December meeting, and Dermott quitted his seat

as Grand Secretary. A meeting of Emergency
was held on the 19th of the same month, when the
names of five Brethren were proposed for the office
of Grand Secretary. Dermott again appealed to
Grand Lodge (against Dickey Junr.) for redress,
and he consented to abide the decision of the
members present. Dermott and Dickey then withdrew. On their return a Minute was read to them,
to the effect that the dispute had been heard, that
Dickey Junr. had been in fault, and that the thanks
of Grand Lodge were given to Dermott.

At a Grand *Committee* held Jan. 30, 1771, to
make choice of a Grand Master, the Duke of Atholl
was chosen. It was announced that Dermott and
a few others had waited upon the Duke of Atholl,
who had expressed his willingness to accept the
office. A deputation was then appointed to wait
upon his Grace and thank him. It was resolved to
meet in future at the *Half Moon* Tavern, Cheapside. Br. W. Dickey Junr. proposed that Dermott
be recommended to the Duke of Atholl for the
office of Deputy Grand Master.

The Grand Lodge was held at the *Half Moon*
Tavern, March 2, 1771, and the Duke of Atholl *
was installed Grand Master. " Laurence Dermott
was installed D^{y.} G^{d.} Mr.," and it is recorded that at

---

* John, third Duke. Henceforth, the Grand Lodge of the
"Antients" was known and distinguished as the " *Atholl*"
Grand Lodge.

the close of the business the Duke gave the Brethren a " Grand feast."

On the 6th of the same month Dermott occupied the chair as Deputy Grand Master for the first time. Br. W. Dickey, Junr. was elected Grand Secretary, and was duly installed into his office ; and then follows the record :—

‚" Here end the Minutes taken by Lau. Dermott, G.S.
From the year 1751
to the year   1771."

It is interesting here to note that, at a Grand Lodge held Sept. 4, 1771, the Grand Secretary Dickey complained of the many flagrant abuses of that most sacred part of Masonry, " The Royal Arch ;" and he proposed that the Masters and Past-Masters of warranted Lodges should be convened as soon as possible, to put this part of Masonry on a solid basis. Their report of the enquiries into these abuses was given at the following meeting in December. It stated that a number of Brethren had been scandalously passed through the Chair, in order to qualify them for the Royal Arch. It was resolved in future no person shall be made a Royal Arch Mason but the legal Representatives of the Lodge, " except a Brother going abroad who hath been twelve months a registered Mason, and must have the unanimous voice of his Lodge." Further consideration was referred to Grand Chapter.

Dermott continued in the office of Deputy Grand
Master until 1774, frequently occupying the Chair.
On the 7th December in that year Grand Secretary
Dickey announced the death of the Grand Master,
the Duke of Atholl. On the 25th of February
following, at a meeting of the Grand Master's
Lodge, his nephew, John, fourth Duke of Atholl,
" was admitted into the First, Second and Third
Degrees, and after proper instructions had been
given," he was installed Master of the Grand
Master's Lodge. On the 1st of March, 1775, he
was elected Grand Master, and on the 25th of the
same month, in the presence of the Duke of
Leinster, G.M. of Ireland, and Sir James Oughton,
Past G.M. of Scotland, his Grace was duly installed.
His first act was to appoint " Brother Laurence
Dermott, Esqre· . . . to be His Grace's Deputy, and
ordered that the said Deputy should be installed,
whenever his present indisposition would admit
him to attend;" which appears to have been in
September in the same year, when he presided.
On that occasion he laid before Grand Lodge an
important communication from the Grand Secretary
of Scotland, relating to "one Wm. Preston, a Lec-
turer on Masonry in London," who "had used
every art to cause a disunion between the Grand
Lodges of Scotland and England." A very interesting correspondence was read, which is too
long to be entered here. The oft-repeated argu-

ments, which are now familiar to us, in which the claims of the two rival Grand Lodges were respectively urged with great vehemence, are set out at length, and occupy several pages. William Preston's attempt to promote discord between the Grand Lodge (Antients) and Grand Lodge of Scotland was unsuccessful; as at a Grand Lodge held at the *Half Moon*, Cheapside, on March 6, 1776, Dermott being in the Chair, there was " read a letter, dated 5th Feb., 1776, from the Grand Lodge of Scotland . . . . tendering the Grand Lodge of England its cordial support," which letter was acknowledged with thanks and a gold medal to W. Mason, Esq., Grand Sect^y. Scot., &c., &c.

Our Provincial Brethren in Salisbury about this time were in collision with the Moderns. On Dec. 3, 1777, Dermott being in the Chair, it is recorded : " Heard a letter from No. 200, Salisbury, setting forth that a Mr. Dunkerley, P.G.M. under the 'Moderns,' had taken upon him to doubt the legality of their Warrant . . . also the D.G. Master's answer thereto." With reference to Dunkerley, Br. Gould, in his highly instructive and interesting work, " Atholl Lodges," says : " This Brother . . . . was frequently reprimanded by the ' Modern ' Grand Chapter for exceeding the bounds of his office."

Heard D.G.M. (Dermott's) letter to the Duke of Atholl, enclosing letter from No. 200, with the G.M.'s reply ; also a letter enclosing proceedings of

Lodge No. 200, as published in the *Salisbury Journal.*

Heard a letter, No. 174, Southampton, similar to that from No. 200. It was resolved "that thanks be given to D.G.M. Dermott for his attention to this matter, assuring him of their readiness to rescue his character from the false and malicious insinuations of Mr. Dunkerley. His trusty conduct during 26 years entitle him to the favour of all well-wishers of the Antient Craft, as appears by Grand Lodge Transactions from 1751 to this date." On this occasion L. Dermott intimated his intention to resign the office of D.G.M. at next meeting.

A complaint was made of irregular admission of Brethren to the Royal Arch, instigated by a Br. Robinson, "who spoke in most indecent terms of the D.G.M. Dermott, declaring that the Duke of Atholl was not G.M., but only represented so by Deputy Dermott, who signed warrants, &c., &c., to answer his own purposes and deceive members of Grand Lodge." It was ordered that Brs. Robinson and Thomas, of No. 193, appear before the Grand Stewards' Lodge.

On 27th Dec., 1777, Dermott in the Chair: Heard a letter from the Duke of Atholl, accepting again the office of Grand Master, and regretting the retirement of Dermott. The Grand Master having been proclaimed, Dermott made an Oration, expressing his regret that Age, Infirmities, and 26 years' service had constrained him to retire from the office of D.G.M. It was resolved to present him with a gold medal.

When Grand Lodge met in March 1778, Br. Robertson replied to the charge made against him in December last, by declaring that he had been deceived: originally a "Modern" Mason, he had since received a letter from the Modern Grand Lodge, which set forth that the Duke of Atholl was *not* the G.M. of Antient Masons; but he was now convinced of his error. Both parties withdrew. A resolution was passed censuring Robertson; Dermott and Robertson then shook hands and declared themselves in perfect friendship with each other.

In June 1778 Dermott sent £10 to Grand Lodge for the Charity. Although Dickey, D.G.M., usually presided, Dermott was frequently present and took part in the general business of the order. Thus we find, when an election for Grand Secretary was about to take place in March 1779, he moved that every candidate for the office be examined relative to the Lodge and place in which he was made; which resulted in Br. Hockaday, of No. 193, a Quartermaster in the Guards, being declared ineligible for Grand Secretary.

The Quarterly Communication was not held on the usual day, June 7, 1780; neither was the Festival celebrated on St. John Baptist's day, in the

same month. London at the time was greatly dis-
turbed and alarmed by the Lord George Gordon
riots, when Newgate and other public buildings
were burnt.

In December 1781 a letter was received from the
Duke of Atholl, signifying his intention to retire
from the office of Grand Master.

The meetings were now again designated "Grand
Committees." Dermott presided in September 1782,
and on that occasion William Randall, Earl of
Antrim, was elected Grand Master.

A Grand Lodge was held in March 1783,
Dermott in the Chair. A letter from Lord Antrim
was read, in which he conferred the honour of
Deputy Grand Master on Dermott, who then
quitted the Chair, and the Lodge constituted itself
a Grand Committee, to consider the letter. It was
resolved that thanks be sent to his Lordship for his
letter, and "for his Lordship's great attention to the
welfare of the Fraternity, in so judicious a choice
of so respectable and worthy a Deputy, whom the
Grand Lodge accepts with pleasure." The Deputy
Grand Master then resumed the Chair.

An entry in the Transactions, under date 3rd
March, 1784, may be here noted, as it relates to
the present Lodge, No. 19. It is as follows : "The
Master and Wardens of Lodge No. 159, having
informed Grand Lodge they had made, entered
and raised seven Brothers whom they found

Worthy and of good Report, and also that the s^{d.} Brors were uncertified Masons before they were ent^{d.} and raised in the Lodge No. 159, and prayed leave that the said Brors be registered in the Grand Lodge Books." Ordered, "that the said Brothers" whose names follow "be registered."

A Grand Lodge of Emergency was held in March 1784, Dermott in the Chair, and sundry matters were discussed and disposed of. The Lodge then resolved itself into a Grand Committee, and Br. Dickey took the Chair. The Grand Secretary read a letter from the R.W.D.G.M. Dermott. It contains a series of complaints and personal rebukes; and charges Leslie, Grand Secretary (elected March 1783), with having exceeded his duties on many occasions, and to have encroached upon the prerogatives of the D.G.M. Dermott having handed in a list containing 19 queries, based on the said letter, retired with Leslie. The Grand Committee deliberated thereon, and finally supported Dermott on all the points of law involved in the dispute, but excused Leslie of having done wrong otherwise than by misconception. Dermott and Leslie were called in, and the result communicated to them, to which they respectively assented.

An angry meeting took place in Sept. 1784. Dermott being in the Chair, informed the Grand Lodge "that he would not act . . . . with the present Gd. Sect^y· .... who, if re-elected, he would ask leave of the Grd. M. to resign his office!" The Gd. Sect^y· replied in warm terms, declaring the D.G.M.'s conduct was "unmasonical." It was referred to a General Committee, and Leslie being put in nomination for G.S., Dermott quitted the Chair. Leslie having been elected by show of hands, declined to act. Another election took place, and Sinclair was elected, but declined. Dermott was requested to resume the Chair, which, being done, the Lodge was closed.

About this time (1774) the meetings of Grand Lodge were very noisy and inharmonious, much anger and acrimonious feeling being displayed on all sides. The irregularity of the proceedings appears to have worried Dermott, who was an earnest advocate for a strict observance of the laws and regulations of Grand Lodge. He saw resolutions made and unmade, elections and re-elections, and a total want of Order existing; added to which, he was in frequent ill-health. In December 1784 he sent a letter to Grand Lodge, in which he said :—

" The only business which you can do with propriety this day is to proclaim the Grand Master and Officers elect, leaving the Installation until a future day. I am not officially acquainted with the proceedings of the last meeting, but from what I have learned they were erroneous, in attempting to rescind the confirmed acts of a Grand Lodge in due form (Sept. 1). It is amazing !!! that amongst such a number of Officers, Old Masons, and even Candidates for the Secretaryship, none sh^d. be found to point out the Futility of such a measure, or remember the difference between a Grand Lodge in *form*—a Grand Lodge in *due form*—and a Grand Lodge in *ample form;* terms so materially significant, defined and useful in the general government of the Fraternity, as to have been constantly observed and continued amongst the Craft in this Kingdom for upwards of 858 years. It requires but a moderate share of Common Sense to know that no Act, Law, Regulation, Order or Decree can be reversed or rescinded nor repealed without a power equal to that by which it was first made and confirmed." He then maintains that the choice of officers made and confirmed by the Grand Lodge in *due form* could not be rescinded by a Grand Lodge only in *form*, without a particular communication from the Grand Master. "For the truth of this see Doct^r. Anderson's Constitutions, page 162, pub. 1738. De Assigny, p. 56, pub. 1744. Spratt's Cons. Reg. 14, pub. 1754, and Ahiman Rez. 14, pub. in 1756, 1764 and 1778. Furthermore, suppose the last G.L. of Dec. 1 was a G.L. in *due form*, or what is much more, a G.L. in *ample form* (his Lordship presiding), I say in such case the G.L. could not rescind nor Repeal any Rule, Order or Decree made and confirmed by a former G.L. (in due or ample form) without giving previous notice thereof in the general summonses, which was not the case on the 1st Dec.ʳ last. . . . . Hence it is manifest the present G.L. are under an indispensable necessity of proclaiming the E. of Antrim G.M. elect (with choice of Deputy)." He then points out how and when objections may be properly made, and concludes : " Thus it is that Justice may be obtained and harmony continued, without endangering the Constitution or even giving a just cause of offence to any party. That Health, Prosperity and Unanimity may attend all and each of you, is the earnest wish of, R.W. and W. Brethren,—Your most sincere friend and very obedt. servant, Lau : Dermott, D.G.M."

The letter was read over several times, and a long silence ensued. A vote of censure was then passed on Dermott, in which his conduct is denounced as " arbitrary, if not altogether illegal."

" Jan. 31, 1785.—G.L. (summoned by Lau. Dermott, Esq., D.G.M.) by authority of G.M. Antrim, at the *Horns* Tavern, Doctors Commons." Dermott in the Chair. There were renewed disputes respecting the Gd. Sect's accounts, which G.L. approved, but which Dermott condemned ; and " the matter dropt without any motion being made thereupon." The next matter named in the summons was the Installation of Grand Officers ; and there being a vote of

censure of the G.L. on the D.G.M., he quitted
the Chair, which was filled by another Brother.
Dermott explained that on account of his illness
he had been unable to obtain the documents sooner
from the G.M., "and as it was ever his wish to
guide them in the path of duty, and not to mis-
guide them nor insult them, he then withdrew."
A discussion followed, and it was moved and
carried that the Censure upon the D.G.M. be now
removed. The D.G.M. returned into the Lodge
and was informed thereof. He returned thanks,
and said he would visit the G.L. as often as he
could, but he declined the office of D.G.M., declaring again "he would not work with the G.
Sect^{y.} &c., &c.; upon which the G.L. got into
confusion and disorder for some time." Some other
business was discussed, and the D.G.M. then closed
the Lodge.

On 2nd March, 1785, the Lodge was opened by
deputation from the R.W.D.G.M. Grand Secretary
Leslie retired from his office, and Br. McCormick
was elected in his place.

A full Grand Lodge was held on the 7th June,
1785, at the *Paul's Head*, Cateaton Street, to which
tavern it was now removed, Dermott being in the
chair. Opened in due form. Procession having
been formed, the Earl of Antrim entered, and with
much circumstance and ceremony was received and
saluted with all the usual honours, "and in due

H

time (after the manner of the G.M. of Israel) solemnly installed in Solomon's Chair and proclaimed." The Grand Lodge was then changed to *ample form.*

At the following meeting the D.G.M. ordered that " a Grand Lodge of Emergency be summoned to meet him on the 29th September," on which day they met at the *Paul's Head,* Dermott in the Chair. It was ordered that the Pursuivant and Tyler shall wear their Cloaks ; one of the resolutions being " Thanks to D.G.M. Dermott, for his condescension in giving up his property of Ahiman Rezon to the Charity."

At this time Dermott continually presided over Grand Lodge, and we find him attending the march out on the Feast of St. John in June 1786, when it is recorded that the D.G.M. and other Grand Officers met at 9 a.m., " at the sign of the *Black Prince,* Newington, with all the respectable Lodges throughout the Cities of London and Westminster, and formed on the Bowling Green for procession to Camberwell Church, and heard an excellent Sermon on the occasion, preached by the Rev. Dr. Colin Milne, and after divine service proceeded to the *Grove House,* Camberwell, and dined in usual form, and drank the toasts . . . "

It is probable the feast was not regarded as an entire success, for at the following meeting it was resolved that " Gd. Lodge should form a mode for the better conducting all Publick processions;" nevertheless, there was a vote of thanks to " R.W. L. Dermott, Esqre. D.G.M., for his good government and masonical abilities." .

At a Grand Lodge held on St. John's-day, December 27, 1787, Dermott in the Chair; by the recommendation of Dermott to the Grand Master, the R.W.J.G.W., James Perry, Esq., was installed as D.G.M. It was resolved "that the thanks of the G.L. be given to the R.W. Lau: Dermott, Esq., Past D.G.M., who, after 47 years zealously and successfully devoted to the service of the Craft, had now retired from the Eminent Station which he held, and to whose masonic knowledge and abilities, inflexible adherence to the Antient Laws of the Fraternity, and impartial administration of Office, the Fraternity are so much indebted." It was also resolved " That a Committee be formed, consisting of the Grand Officers, to consider the best means of conferring some signal mark of the approbation of the G.L. on the said Mr. Deputy Dermott, and report to the G.L."

March 4, 1789.—Dermott presented a memorial against the proceedings of No. 5 Lodge, but as the Brethren of that Lodge had not been apprised thereof, it was postponed. This seems to have been the last occasion on which Dermott was present in Grand Lodge. The memorial was heard and considered at a Grand Lodge held on June

3, 1789, when, after mutual explanations, it was amicably and finally settled.

Thus ends the record of this remarkable Mason. We learn nothing more of him in the Grand Lodge books. Doubtless age and failing health caused him to withdraw from the field of his more active labours. For some years he had resided in King Street, Tower Hill, but he subsequently removed to Mile End, where, with his wife, he remained until his death, which took place in June 1791.

The zeal and success with which he devoted a large portion of his life to the service of the Craft; the many battles which he fought against her enemies within and without; his staunch and inflexible adherence to the ancient landmarks of the Order, and the vast knowledge which he brought to bear upon his work, justly entitled him not only to the encomiums which his Grand Lodge pronounced upon him, but to the generous admiration of his Brethren in succeeding ages.

And so we drop the veil over LAU : DERMOTT.

APPENDIX.

THE WILL OF LAURENCE DERMOTT.

(In the Prerogative Court of Canterbury.)

In the Name of God, Amen. I, Laurence Dermott, of the Parish of Saint Botolph, Aldgate, in the County of Middlesex, Wine Merchant, being of sound mind and memory, make this my last Will and Testament. Item, I bequeath my immortal Soul to the immortal Creator of all things, my body to the earth; and all my worldly riches I bequeath to my dearly beloved wife, Elizabeth Dermott, whom I appoint my whole and sole Executrix of this my last Will and Testament, the fifth day of June in the year of our Lord one thousand seven hundred and seventy.

LAU : DERMOTT. (L. S.)

Signed and sealed in the presence of
Wm. Whittaker.
Frans. Allen.
Willm. Smith.

Proved at London, 15 July, 1791, before the Worshipful Thomas Bevor, Doctor of Laws and Surrogate, by the Oath of Elizabeth Dermott, Widow, the Relict, the sole Executrix named in the said Will, to whom Admon was granted, having been first sworn duly to administer.

The Testator was formerly of St. Botolph, Aldgate, but late of Mile End Old Town, in the Parish of St. Dunstan, Stepney, and he died last month.

TO THE READER.

The writer has devoted considerable time and labour in an attempt to discover Dermott's burial place, and he will be very much obliged to any one who will give him information on the subject.

As a guide to fellow-labourers in the search, the following facts may be stated :—

Laurence Dermott died in June 1791.

His last known residence was in Mile End Old Town, Stepney.

The following Registers have been searched:

> **St. Botolph, Aldgate.**
> **Christ Church, Spitalfields.**
> **St. Mary, Bow.**
> **St. Mary, Bromley (Middx.)**
> **St. Anne, Limehouse.**
> **St. Dunstan, Stepney.**
> **St. Mary, Whitechapel.**
> **Bunhill Fields.**
> **Bull Lane.**